P9-BYK-911

Flossmoor Public Library
1000 Sterling Avenue
Flossmoor, IL 60422-1295
Phone: (708) 798-3600

ENDANGERED ANIMALS

POLAR BEARS

Flossmoor Public Library
1000 Sterling Avenue
Flossmoor, IL 60422-1295
(708) 798-3600

BY SHERYL PETERSON

The Child's World

Published by The Child's World®
1980 Lookout Drive • Mankato, MN 56003-1705
800-599-READ • www.childsworld.com

Acknowledgments
The Child's World®: Mary Berendes, Publishing Director
Red Line Editorial: Editorial direction and production
The Design Lab: Design
Amnet: Production

Design Element: Shutterstock Images
Photographs ©: Susanne Miller/U.S. Fish and Wildlife
Service, cover, 1, 11; iStockphoto, 4; John Pitcher/
iStockphoto, 6–7; Elliot Hurwitt/iStockphoto, 8; U.S. Fish
and Wildlife Service, 9, 22; Howard Perry/iStockphoto, 10;
Vladimir Melnik/Shutterstock Images, 13; Shutterstock
Images, 15; Sergey Uryadnikov/Shutterstock Images, 16,
20–21; Karyn Rode/U.S. Fish and Wildlife Service, 17;
Jenny E. Ross/Corbis, 19

Copyright © 2016 by The Child's World®
All rights reserved. No part of this book may be reproduced
or utilized in any form or by any means without written
permission from the publisher.

ISBN 9781631439704
LCCN 2014959640

Printed in the United States of America
Mankato, MN
July, 2015
PA02264

ABOUT THE AUTHOR

Sheryl Peterson lives in International Falls, Minnesota. Her town's nickname is "Icebox of the Nation." But it is not cold enough for polar bears! Peterson has written 23 nonfiction books for kids, including an award-winning picture book.

TABLE OF CONTENTS

CHAPTER ONE

SNOW BEAR, SEA BEAR

This polar bear's white fur helps it blend in with the snow.

Polar bears are the largest bears in the world. They have dazzling white fur. Native **Arctic** people call the polar bear "nanuk." It means wise and powerful.

Every fall in Canada, a chilly north wind starts to blow. When it does, polar bears gather on Hudson Bay near Churchill, Manitoba. That town is called the "Polar Bear Capital of the World." Polar bears gather and wait for the sea

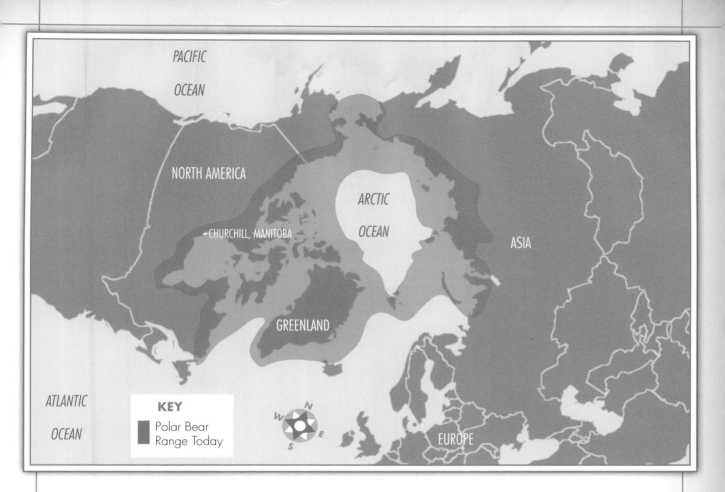

Polar bears live in the Arctic, near the North Pole.

ice to form. They leave land as soon as the ice is thick enough to hold them. The bears travel for hundreds of miles across the ice. They are hungry and searching for food.

Polar bears are meat eaters. They hunt ringed or bearded seals. Polar bears need seal fat to live. The bears climb onto floating ice platforms to hunt. They have excellent hearing and

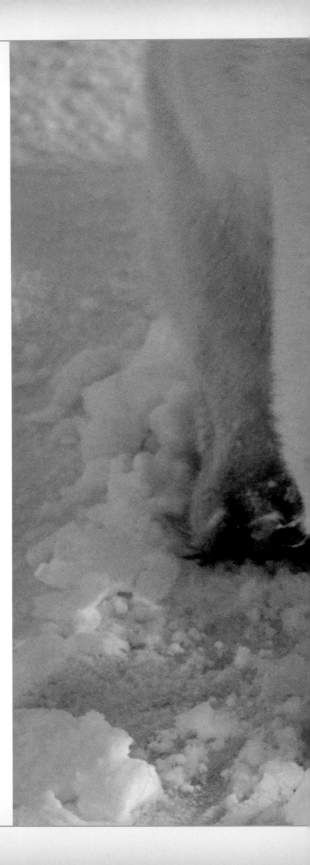

an excellent sense of smell. The bears can sniff out a seal's den. They can find a seal's breathing hole in the ice. They can find the holes from more than 1 mile (1.6 km) away. The bears may watch a breathing hole for hours before catching a seal.

Well-fed, healthy male polar bears can weigh up to 2,000 pounds (907 kg). They can measure almost 10 feet (3 m) long. Female polar bears are about half that size. Polar bears have big feet. They spread their paws out wide like snowshoes. This helps them

This polar bear has found a seal breathing hole in the ice.

stay on top of the snow. Polar bears have short claws and tiny grippers on the pads of their feet. The claws and grippers dig into the slippery ice. This helps polar bears stay on their feet.

Polar bears spend much of their time on the ice. But often, they need to swim to find food. They are super swimmers. They paddle with their broad, slightly webbed front feet. They use their back feet to steer. Their oily fur coat repels water

Polar bears have short claws they use to grip the ice.

easily. It helps the bears float. A fat layer under their skin keeps them warm.

Most polar bears do not **hibernate** in winter. But pregnant female polar bears do. They dig dens in the snow in the fall. Polar bear cubs are born deep in the snow den. They are born

Polar bear cubs leave their dens in early spring.

between December and February. The cubs look like small, hairless guinea pigs. They are almost always twins or triplets. The mother nurses the cubs in the den for three or four months. She eats no food during this time. She must depend on her stored body fat.

In late March, mother and baby polar bears pop out of the den. The cubs stay in their mother's care for about two years. Like adult bears, they have black skin to **absorb** the sun's rays. Their white fur works as **camouflage** in the ice and snow. After they turn two, polar bears are ready to live on their own.

These two cubs are nearly large enough to live on their own.

CHAPTER TWO

HARM TO HABITAT

Polar bears face several threats, all from human activities.

Polar bears have no natural **predators**. But polar bears are still in danger. Human activities are the biggest threat to the bears. Today there are approximately 20,000 to 25,000 wild polar bears. Their numbers are going down.

Before 1973, hunters killed many polar bears. That year, the five nations with land bordering the Arctic Sea signed a **treaty**. It banned polar bear hunting for most people. But native Arctic people are still allowed to hunt the bears. Doing so is part of their culture and tradition. Native Arctic people eat polar bear meat. They use the animals' furry skins to make warm snow pants and soft boots.

Climate change is another threat to polar bears. It is destroying the bears' **habitat**. The earth's average temperature

Arctic ice has shrunk between 1980 and 2014.

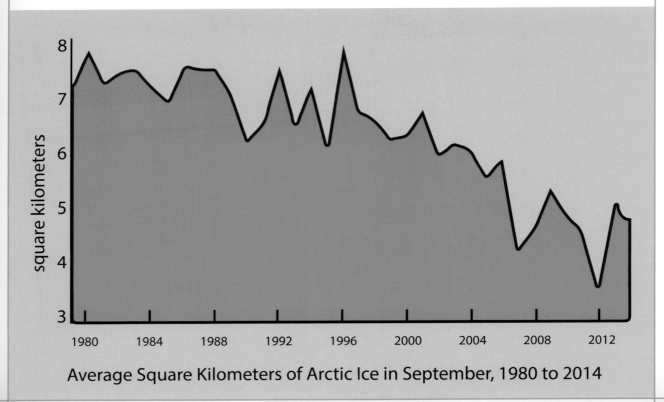

Average Square Kilometers of Arctic Ice in September, 1980 to 2014

Shrinking sea ice puts polar bears at risk.

is getting warmer. This has caused the ice in the Arctic to start to melt. Every year it melts faster. It breaks up and falls into the ocean. This affects polar bears. They have a difficult time traveling and finding food without ice to float on. Without food, the bears struggle to raise their young. Some bears even starve to death.

Without sea ice to rest on while hunting, some polar bears drown. Lack of ice forces the bears to spend more time on land. On land, they are more likely to run into humans. Sometimes bears near towns look in garbage cans for food. They are not naturally afraid of humans. If humans feel threatened, they may kill the bears.

As the sea ice melts, oil companies can access more water. They set up huge drills in the ocean. The drills need barges, oil tankers, and cargo ships to operate. These activities disturb the bears.

Harmful chemicals also threaten polar bears. Chemicals from farms, sewage, ships, and factories float in the water up to the Arctic. There, small fish may absorb them. Those fish are eaten by larger fish. Seals eat the larger fish. Then polar bears eat the seals. All the while, the chemicals build up in the

OIL AND WATER

An average of 450 oil and other spills occur in northern Alaska yearly. These spills are dangerous for polar bears. Eating just a small amount of oil can cause death. Oil spills damage dens, killing cubs. People have not found a good way to clean oil off sea ice.

animals. The chemicals build up and become more harmful. Eating the toxic seals can hurt even a strong polar bear.

Polar bears can handle the dangers of extreme cold. But they do not know how to deal with human-made dangers. Humans must protect polar bears from these dangers to help the bears' numbers grow.

Polar bears need human help to survive in the wild.

CHAPTER THREE

WORLD RESCUE

Scientists search for polar bear dens in spring.

Polar bears are considered to be **vulnerable**. Many human activities threaten these animals. But many people work to protect the bears, too. Scientists around the world study polar bears. In March and April, the bears become more active. So do the scientists. They ride snowmobiles over icy land to search for bear dens. Some scientists scan the area from helicopters. Researchers count the dens and compare the total to the year before.

Sometimes scientists safely **tranquilize** polar bears and weigh them. They check to see if the bears are getting enough

This scientist is giving a tranquilized polar bear a checkup.

to eat. Other bears are fitted with radio collars to track their travels. Scientists can see changes in a bear's daily life or in the sea ice of a region. They try to do these tests without stressing the bears too much.

Arctic communities work to separate polar bears from people so that both are safe. Towns install good lighting. This helps people spot polar bears. People also install electric fences. These help keep bears out of public places. Residents also use bear-proof food storage containers.

Many bears wait on land for the ice to thicken in Churchill, Manitoba, each fall. There are so many that they roam the streets. Citizens there form bear patrol groups. They watch for the bears and use loud noises to keep them away.

POLAR BEAR WEEK

Every November, Polar Bear International celebrates Polar Bear Week. It occurs around the time bears turn up at Churchill. The group teaches people how to help polar bears. They provide videos for people to learn more about polar bears.

A polar bear looks for food in a Churchill landfill while it waits for sea ice to form.

People around the world form groups to help protect polar bears. They raise money to help the bears. They tell others about the serious problem of melting sea ice. One group, Polar Bears International, has a plan called SOS! These letters stand for "Save Our Sea Ice." The plan brings attention to the effect climate change has on polar bears. Polar Bears International has an online webcam. People can watch video of the bears gathering on land in the fall. And an online tracker map lets people follow the bears' travels.

Polar bears are one of the Arctic's wild treasures. Humans continue to work together to learn more about these bears. They find ways to protect the bears' icy habitat.

With human help, polar bears can continue to enjoy their icy habitat.

WHAT YOU CAN DO

- Make a donation to a group that protects polar bears.

- Celebrate International Polar Bear Day on February 27 by learning more about polar bears' Arctic habitat.

- Plan a "Pedal for Polar Bears" event to raise money to help the bears.

- Learn all you can about polar bears, and share what you know with your friends.

GLOSSARY

absorb (ab-SORB) To absorb is to take something in, such as a liquid. Fish absorb chemicals in ocean water.

Arctic (ARK-tik) The Arctic is the frozen area around the North Pole. Polar bears live in the extreme cold of the Arctic.

camouflage (KAM-uh-flahzh) Camouflage is a color or covering that helps an animal blend in with its surroundings. A polar bear's white coat is camouflage against the white snow.

climate change (KLYE-mit CHANJ) Climate change is a term for significant, long-term changes in Earth's temperature, wind patterns, and rain and snowfall totals. Climate change affects polar bears' habitat.

habitat (HAB-i-tat) A habitat is a place in nature where animals or plants live. The Arctic is polar bears' habitat.

hibernate (HIE-bur-nayt) To hibernate is to pass a length of time in a resting state. Only mother polar bears hibernate.

predators (PRED-a-terz) Predators hunt, kill, and eat other animals. Polar bears do not have natural predators.

tranquilize (TRANG-kwuhl-ize) To tranquilize an animal is to put it to sleep for a period of time. Scientists tranquilize polar bears to study them.

treaty (TREE-tee) A treaty is an agreement between countries. The five Arctic nations signed a treaty to protect polar bears.

vulnerable (VUL-nur-uh-bul) Something that is vulnerable is open to danger or harm. Polar bears are considered to be vulnerable.

TO LEARN MORE

BOOKS

Castaldo, Nancy F., and Karen de Seve. *Mission: Polar Bear Rescue*. Washington, DC: National Geographic Kids, 2014.

Newman, Mark. *Polar Bears*. New York: Henry Holt, 2011.

Orr, Tamra. *Polar Bears*. New York: Scholastic, 2013.

WEB SITES

Visit our Web site for links about polar bears:
childsworld.com/links

Note to Parents, Teachers, and Librarians: We routinely verify our Web links to make sure they are safe and active sites. So encourage your readers to check them out!

INDEX